Secrets

of

Progress

& ENLARGEMENT

DR. D. K. OLUKOYA

Secrets of Progress and Enlargement

ISBN: 978-978-920-050-4

Published 2014

Published by:
The Battle Cry Christian Ministries
322, Herbert Macaulay Street, Sabo, Yaba
P. O. Box 12272, Ikeja, Lagos.
www.battlecrystore.com
email: info@battlecrystore.com
        customercare@battlecrystore.com
        sales@battlecrystore.com
Phone: 0803-304-4239, 0816-122-9775

I salute my wonderful wife, Pastor Shade, for her invaluable support in the ministry.

I appreciate her unquantifiable support in the book ministry as the cover designer, art editor and art adviser.

All the Scriptures are from the King James Version

C O N T E N T S

▶ CHAPTER 1

Secrets of Progress & ENLARGEMENT

GOD OF NEWNESS

The God of Rehoboth is the God of new things, new beginnings. God is a God of newness and freshness. God is a God of creation, innovation and energy. God is so creative that He does not have to do the same thing in the same way. He has an infinite way, He can do His own thing in the world.

Many a time you limit God because you confine Him with the level of your brain. In the book of Genesis, God gave an old woman a boy. God told Abraham that He was going to make a nation out of him. Abraham tried all he could to make a nation but he could not. Abraham thought God was going to use his servant, but God used an old woman to give birth to the son who would be a father of nations.

> *For all the wells which his father's servants had digged in the days of Abraham his father, the Philistines had stopped them, and filled them*

with earth. And Abimelech said unto Isaac, Go from us; for thou art much mightier than we. And Isaac departed thence, and pitched his tent in the valley of Gerar, and dwelt there. And Isaac digged again the wells of water, which they had digged in the days of Abraham his father; for the philistines had stopped them after the death of Abraham: and he called their names after the names by which his father had called them. And Isaac's servants digged in the valley, and found there a well of springing water. And the herdmen of Gerar did strive with Isaac's herdmen, saying, The water is ours: and he called the name of the well Esek; because they strove with him. And they digged another well, and strove for that also: and he called the name of it Sitnah. And he removed from thence, and digged another well; and for that they strove not: and he called the name of it Rehoboth; and he said, For now the LORD hath made room for us, and we shall be fruitful in the land. Gen 26:15-22

DIVINE ENLARGEMENT

The above Bible passage makes it clear that Abraham built wells and when it came to Isaac's turn, the Philistines stopped Isaac the son of Abraham, from digging the well. They filled the well with stones. Filling a well in a land that lacks sources of water with stones is a malicious and foolish act.

When Isaac dug the well, the Philistines came and took the well from him and Isaac named the well Esek. The Philistines also cheated Isaac when he dug another well, which they took from him. Isaac also named the second well, Sitnah He named the two wells, Esek and Sitnah because they strove with him over the wells. But when Isaac dug well, which he named Rehoboth, the Philistines did not strive with him.

In the scriptures, 'well' means 'dependence'. The enemy blocking the well, are actually stopping the flow of parental and ancestral blessings. Isaac dug his well and he named the well Esek, which means dispute and contention. He dug another well which the Philistine took from him, and he called the well, Sitnah. For the third time he dug another well and the Philistines did not strive with him and he named the well Rehoboth.

God does things that people open their mouth and gaze at what He has done. In the book of Exodus, God did a new thing. He divided the Red Sea. God controlled the sea. God rained manna from heaven. God brought down the walls of Jericho with a shout and no weapon. God is a God of new things.

When Jesus Christ came into the scene He began to do new things He had never done before. Jesus walked on water. He fed multitudes with just a small quantity of food.

2Sam 22:20

> *He brought me forth also into a large place: he delivered me, because he delighted in me.*

Psalm 118:29

> *O give thanks unto the LORD; for he is good: for his mercy endureth for ever.*

Rehoboth means a wide place. It means plenty of room to live. Rehoboth means conditions that make you to stay and prosper.

God is a God of Rehoboth. God of Rehoboth means, God who makes room. God of Rehoboth is a God that calms the raging sea. God of Rehoboth is the God that silences the raging of the enemy. The Bible says in the beginning, God created the heavens and the earth. The earth was without form and void and darkness was upon the face of the deep. There was plenty of confusion, but the spirit of God moved upon the waters.

There was a lot of confusion, shapelessness until the voice of God said, let there be light.

GOD OF ENLARGEMENT

The God of Rehoboth is the God of restoration. No matter what you have lost, the God of Rehoboth shall restore it. The God of Rehoboth is the God of enlargement and faithfulness. The God of Rehoboth is the God Who gives rest. The The God of Rehoboth is the God of uncommon prosperity. God of Rehoboth is a God of profitable relocation.

Isaac never knew that they were pushing him towards his breakthroughs. The enemies made a mistake and pushed Isaac into the place of his promotion. The God of Rehoboth is the God of breakthrough. He is the God who silences thieves. The God of Rehoboth is the God who rewards persistence. He rewards people who do not give up. Isaac kept digging wells until he got to his place of breakthroughs. The God of Rehoboth is the God who hates poverty. The God of

Rehoboth is the God who never forgets His own people. The God of Rehoboth makes you to find water on dry ground. The God of Rehoboth makes a way where men say there is no way.

MAJOR HINDERANCES

There are many hindrances in answering prayers, but the two major hindrances to prayers are:

1. **Unbelief:** When you lack faith. When you do not believe in God's agenda for your life.
2. **Sin:** Sin can shorten the hands of God from touching your life. You do not have to get involved in hypocrisy because it will endanger your life.

Unbelief and sin are blessing blockers to your life. You need to restrain yourself from anger and ill-temper because it will hinder your blessings from God. God of Rehoboth will bless you abundantly if you do everything he says to you and your life will take a new turn.

Prayer Points ⟵——————————

1. Power working against my favour, your time is up, die, in the name of Jesus.
2. Every power blocking my forward movement, die, in the name of Jesus.
3. Buried blessings belonging to me, arise and locate me, in the name of Jesus.
4. Witchcraft birds assigned against my portion die, in the name of Jesus.
5. Every judgement of darkness against my head, scatter, in the name of Jesus.
6. My life, hear the word of the Lord, arise and shine by fire, in the name of Jesus.
7. Every power mentioning my name in the dark, you are a liar, die, in the name of Jesus.
8. Every idol from my place of birth, that is swallowing my virtues, vomit them and die, in the name of Jesus.
9. Demotion yokes, break by fire, in Jesus' name.
10. Eaters of flesh and drinkers of blood, my life is not your candidate, therefore, die, in the name of Jesus.

CHAPTER 2

The
Mystery
of
FAILURE

Some years ago in England, the fire brigade went on strike and the army had to replace them for the time being. So when anybody needed help, they would call the Army. There was a woman whose cat climbed on top of a tree and could not come down. She called the fire brigade and the soldier boys went there and rescued the cat professionally.

The old woman was very happy and she offered them a cup of coffee and biscuit and after they had taken the coffee and biscuits, on their way back, as they drove their car, they mistakenly crushed the rescued cat to death. They failed woefully after they had succeeded. There is a mystery about failure. When bright men become failures and the ones that are supposed to be hardworking receive the arrow of laziness, there is a mystery somewhere.

Phil 3:14-15

> *I press toward the mark for the prize of the high calling of God in Christ Jesus. Let us therefore, as many as be*

perfect, be thus minded: and if in any thing ye be otherwise minded, God shall reveal even this unto you.

I pray that right now the arrows of failure tormenting your life will go back to the sender. Yesterday is a cancelled cheque, tomorrow is a promissory note but today is the only thing you have and you must utilise it.

HARD FACTS ABOUT FAILURE

1. **You are not a failure until you are satisfied being one.** The Bible says, that you shall be the head and not the tail.
2. **The cost of failure is greater than the price of success.**
3. **The worst failure is failure to try.** There is no harm in trial. Anything that is binding the hand of a man from trying is an agent of the devil
4. **If you have no enemy you are a celebrated failure.** The Bible says, "Let God arise and let his enemies be scattered". We all know that it is the tree that bears

sweet fruits that people throw stones at. Nobody throws stones at an unproductive tree.

5. **If you think small, you stay small.** The Bible says, as a man thinketh in his heart, so is he.

6. **If you lie on the ground, you cannot fall lower.** If you fall and do not have appetite to rise again, you are a qualified failure.

7. **Failure is the only thing that can be achieved without much efforts.**

8. **No man is a failure until he is a failure from the inside.** I pray that any internal yoke that has limited your life be scattered in the mighty name of Jesus. Amen.

9. **The greatest loneliness is the loneliness of failure.** A failure is a stranger in his own house. When there is a family meeting and people are making contributions, when a failure raises up his hands to speak, he is silenced immediately. He therefore becomes a stranger, even to his family members.

10. **Every unfriendly person is a failure.**

WHAT IS FAILURE?

1. Failure is to fall short of success.
2. Failure is to fall short of achievements.
3. Failure is to score lower than the passing grade or mark.

In the school of failure there are grades. Failure implies a total defeat. Biblically failure is an inability to plunge yourself into your divine destiny. It is to be less than what God expects of you. When you achieve less than what you should, you are a failure. There are millionaires that are failures, because they are supposed to be billionaires.

Failure leads to frustration, anger, hatred, confusion and bitterness. God's plan is always perfect. But a good idea might not be a God's idea. God's plans are always perfect. Man fails because of imperfection. I pray that every agenda of failure assigned against your life shall be buried alive.

REASONS FOR FAILURE

1. **LEAVING GOD OUT OF YOUR CALCULATIONS.** Once a man has no restraint from certain acts, he is a failure. When God is not directing the affairs of a man, the man is a total failure.

2. **LACK OF VISION.** Some people fail because they have no plan for their lives and they do not even know that they have failed. The Bible says that without vision the people perish.

Pro 29:18

> *Where there is no vision, the people perish: but he that keepeth the law, happy is he.*

3. **INNADEQUATE TRAINING:** People who are not trained in what they are supposed to do often fail.

4. **MIS-PLACED GIIFTS.** Some people are gifted in one area, but they are not interested in developing and using their gifts. They go to another thing that they are not gifted at and this leads to failure. This accounts for a great percentage of failure in schools and in several professional lines.

5. **UNWILLINGNESS TO PAY THE PRICE.** If a man is not ready to pay the price of success, he gets failure free of charge. Anything good has a price.

6. **PRAYERLESSNESS.** When you embark on a task without consulting God and seeking his face, you are fishing in the ocean of failure. One of the biggest problems in the body of Christ is prayerlessness. Many christians have run helter skelter to places they should not even visit and this has caused a lot of insult to christendom.

7.   **LACK OF EVALUTION.** When a believer is not checking his or her life very well, failure sets in.

8.   **FEAR.** A fearful person cannot make progress. The Bible says that God has not given us the spirit of fear but of power, of love and of a sound mind. Fear can make someone misbehave, backslide and die. I bind every spirit of fear in your life in the name of Jesus.

9.   **DOUBT.** When you doubt what God can do for you, and you underestimate the power of God to change a particular situation in your life, it is a direct admission into the school of failure.

10.   **PROCRASTINATION.** When you wait too much for a better time to do a particular thing, that best time might never come. Procrastination is the ancestor of failure.

11. **EXCUSES.** Giving excuses is like justifying your failure instead of correcting it. God has a perfect hatred for excuses. God punctured all the excuses of Moses and when he said he could not talk, God asked him to use Aaron. There is always a way to do a thing, instead of giving excuses.

12. **LAZINESS.** This is resting when you are not tired. Most people who claim to be christians are very lazy. Some men even sit down at home and wait for their wives to bring food for them. Some will say that they are bigger than a particular job and they would refuse to work. This is laziness and pride. There was a woman, who lost her job and she came to me that I should give her 2,500 and pray on it. I did as she demanded and she started selling biscuits. Few months later, she came with a tithe of 50,000. Laziness is an enemy of progress. This also accounts for the reason women sell their bodies for money.

13.   **SELFISHNESS.** Selfish people fail because in their stinginess, they encounter trouble. The most prosperous people on earth are those who have the interest of others at heart. It is not what you recieve that makes you rich, but what you give out.

Luke 6:38

> *Give, and it shall be given unto you; good measure, pressed down, and shaken together, and running over, shall men give into your bosom. For with the same measure that ye mete withal it shall be measured to you again.*

Acts 20:35

> *I have shewed you all things, how that so labouring ye ought to support the weak, and to remember the words of the Lord Jesus, how he said, It is more blessed to give than to receive.*

14. **DISUNITY.** Disunity provides a fertile ground for abysmal failure. There is power in unity.

Psalm 133:1

> *Behold, how good and how pleasant it is for brethren to dwell together in unity!*

Eph 4:3

> *Endeavouring to keep the unity of the Spirit in the bond of peace.*

Eph 4:13

> *Till we all come in the unity of the faith, and of the knowledge of the Son of God, unto a perfect man, unto the measure of the stature of the fulness of Christ:*

15. **DISOBEDIENCE.** When you erect your destiny structure on the platform of disobedience, you have already failed.

Disobedience to God and legally constituted authority brings failure.

16. **LACK OF GOOD WORKERS.** The success or failure of your organisation or project depends on the calibre of workers involved in it.

17. **DISHONESTY.** Anything that has a foundation of falsehood cannot stand. Dishonesty is a key in the school of failure. Meditate on these words.

Philippians 4:8

> *Finally, brethren, whatsoever things are true, whatsoever things are honest, whatsoever things are just, whatsoever things are pure, whatsoever things are lovely, whatsoever things are of good report; if there be any virtue, and if there be any praise, think on these things.*

18. **FAILURE TO LEARN FROM EXPERIENCE.** When you make a mistake and repeat the mistakes, it leads to failure. This is why they say history repeats itself. It does because people do not learn from experience.

1Cor 10:1-12

Moreover, brethren, I would not that ye should be ignorant, how that all our fathers were under the cloud, and all passed through the sea; And were all baptized unto Moses in the cloud and in the sea; And did all eat the same spiritual meat; And did all drink the same spiritual drink: for they drank of that spiritual Rock that followed them: and that Rock was Christ. But with many of them God was not well pleased: for they were overthrown in the wilderness. Now these things were our examples, to the intent we should not lust after evil things, as they also lusted. Neither be ye idolaters, as were some of them; as it is written, The people sat down to eat and drink, and rose up to play. Neither let us commit fornication, as some of them committed, and fell in one day three and twenty thousand. Neither let us tempt Christ, as some of them also tempted, and were destroyed of serpents. Neither murmur ye, as some of them also murmured, and were destroyed of the destroyer. Now all these things happened unto them for ensamples: and they are written for our admonition, upon whom the ends of the world are come. Wherefore let him that thinketh he standeth take heed lest he fall.

19. **SPIRITUAL ATTACKS.** Spiritual attack from the enemies also lead to failure. Satan brings enemies to the way of a believer to frustrate that believer's attempt to excel in life. This is to understand the principles of spiritual warfare.

Matthew 13:24-30

Another parable put he forth unto them, saying, The kingdom of heaven is likened unto a man which sowed good seed in his field: But while men slept, his enemy came and sowed tares among the wheat, and went his way. But when the blade was sprung up, and brought forth fruit, then appeared the tares also. So the servants of the householder came and said unto him, Sir, didst not thou sow good seed in thy field? from whence then hath it tares? He said unto them, An enemy hath done this.

The servants said unto him, Wilt thou then that we go and gather them up? But he said, Nay; lest while ye gather up the tares, ye root up also the wheat with them. Let both grow together until the harvest: and in the time of harvest I will say to the reapers, Gather ye together first the tares, and bind them in bundles to burn them: but gather the wheat into my barn.

20. **CURSES.** When a curse is upon a person, he will always experience failure. A cursed person may have all the certificates of success, but he will still fail. When he is given the best, he will come out with the worst. It is very important to break every form of curses against excelling in life.

WHAT TO DO, TO BE FREE

1. Evaluate your life.
2. Pray enquirying prayer:-

A.   Father, where am I going wrong?
B.   Father, what should I do?
C.   Father, how should I proceed?

3.   Obey the instruction of God.
4.   Wage war against every satanic agent that causes failure.

Prayer Points ←————————————

1.   Agent of darkness assigned to stop me, I stop you before you stop me, in the name of Jesus.
2.   Yokes of satanic delay, die, in the name of Jesus.
3.   O Lord God of Elijah, arise and move me forward.
4.   Every infirmity assigned to make me fail, I destroy you with fire, in the name of Jesus.
5.   Pillars of witchcraft in my family, die, in the name of Jesus.
6.   Power that does not want new things in my life, you are a liar, die, in the name of Jesus.
7.   Teeth of the enemy over my life, break, in the name of Jesus.

▶ CHAPTER 3

War Against
Capacity
BLOCKERS

1.   Every power assigned to bury me alive, you are a liar, die, in the name of Jesus.
2.   Every power, assigned to rubbish my life, die, in the name of Jesus.
3.   Every antagonising powers, die, in the name of Jesus

If you remain in the tail position, the fault will not be anyone's but yours. It will be your faults, if you are caught trying to kill an elephant with a broom stick. It is a serious matter and I want you to understand the subject matter. The manner of prayers listed above, highlights the importance of the topic. The prayer should be said in the spirit of enough is enough. You should pray, that everything your forefathers have lost and that has been thrown away, you must recover them in your generation. Your prayer should be that, the true picture of your life that God wants you to lived must be restored.

There are some people, who are internal gold mines. But then, the enemy has buried the gold mine in the crucible of frustration and disappointments. There are people who are shining stars, but they are buried in the dung-hill of fear and frustration.

The activity of capacity blockers has assumed an epidemic dimension. Capacity blockers have gone on rampage. Beloved, perhaps, you have not been praying hard, make sure that you do not keep your mouth shut. They say that, "a closed mouth is a closed destiny". If blind Bartimaeus had kept quiet, he would have died a blind man. There are some people, who are supposed to be mountain movers but they cannot move anything, because of capacity blockers. There are some people, who where they are now, was where they were supposed to be 20 years ago. There are people, who should have been divine bankers or partners of the Almighty, but, because they have been tackled to a stand still, they cannot perform.

Proverb 18:16 says;

> *A man's gift maketh room for him, and bringeth him before great men.*

YOUR GIFT

There is a "man's gift", something in your life that has a capacity to make a way for you and bring you before great men. That is the capacity we are talking about in this book.

Psalm 49:20

> *Man that is in honour, and understandeth not, is like the beasts that perish.*

The Bible makes it clear that you are a gold mine. You have a unique capacity, great talents, and wonderful potential but you are completely unaware. It is like the beast that perishes. What a terrible statement! No one is born into the world to just hang around. There are many people hanging around in our world. All of us, the moment you were born, you came crying from your mother's womb, your time began to count; that time does not wait for you. Time is not a friend of anybody. Time waits for nobody. Many people are living but they are not fulfilling their destiny and their maximum capacity. There is a world of difference between living long and living effectively. By thirty three years, Jesus' assignment had finished. By 120 years, Moses had finished his assignment. This is a matter we need to think about. Unto every man brought into the world, there is a divine investment waiting for expression in your life. A divine investment which God has brought you here to trade with and to prosper.

THE SLEEPING GIANT

Deep down, buried inside many, is a sleeping giant that has fallen asleep. Listen, you worth much more than you think. God has put so much into you. One strange tragedy of our world is that there are many people with plenty of valuable virtues lying down dormant in them, unused and unexplored. Pray about your destiny. Pray to wake up your inner giant. It is time to trigger the manifestations of those hidden internal resources. Many have gone to dead churches and have become mesmerised spiritually. They die even more before they come in contact with a living church.

The muscles of the body does not manifest their capacity unless you put them to use and challenge them. Your inner capacity is like those muscles. The hidden abilities, potentials, talents are goldmines. As far as they are hidden, they cannot produce profit. The message is that you need to wage war against those powers that are pulling you down and not allowing you to fulfill that which the Almighty has planted in you.

THE MEANING

What do we mean by capacity? We mean, what you can become but you have not yet realised. In a single seed, there is a tree and there is also a forest. That single seed has a capacity to be a big tree; it also has capacity to become a forest. But if somebody crushes the seed under the feet, the person has blocked that capacity. Capacity is what you can do but have not yet done it. It means where you can go but you have not, yet, gone.

I prophesy that where your enemy says you will not reach, you will not only get there, you will surpass that point in the name of Jesus.

By your capacity we mean your unused strength. The capacity is there but you are not using it. We mean your untapped power. It means your unrealised ability. It means your hidden talent. It means your unrecognised gifts. It means the obscure giant hiding within you. It means your unmanifested breakthrough. It means your unexplained responsibilities. It means your unexpressed ideas. It means your unsung songs, your undanced dance. It means your unwritten books. It refers to your undeclared manifestoes. This is what we mean by capacity.

THE EXPLORATION

Until your capacity is discovered and tapped, greatness will be far. Your capacity is your ability carved out of your divine ability. Your capacity is your limited ideas extracted from the bountiful sea of divine intelligence. Until you decide to dare the impossible, you will continue to be an ordinary person.

> *Every power that wants to trivialise my destiny, be disgraced, in the name of Jesus.*

A man will not be a blessing to his generation until he comes up with a burning desire to release his capacity. There are plenty of people in affliction today because they have not yet discovered what God has given to them. The greatest problems people have is inability to manifest. Your lack of manifestation is causing a lot of restlessness. There are many of us that when our destiny was announced in heaven, the devil shivered. That is why the devil generally troubles every child of destiny. He would quickly arrange any useless girl to truncate the destiny of such a man. The enemy assigns useless boyfriends to a destiny woman. That is why the situation is so bad in our secondary schools, where boyfriends and girlfriends are common. Primary school children are sleeping with themselves in the school toilet.

The enemy arranges sinner boyfriends and useless sinner girlfriends. A boy who does not know what he is going to become in life will be looking for girlfriends who will derail him. The enemy also arranges deficit boyfriends for promising ladies.

When somebody has been derailed, the person needs urgent prayers. Such a person needs to be brought back to the road from which he derailed. Your capacity can be derailed. Your capacity is precious. It is answer to somebody's prayer. Your financial freedom is tied to the release of your capacity. Beloved, when you pray aggressively, the first thing you will notice, is that your dream life will change. You will begin to have destiny dreams. The strategy of the enemy is to distract your attention from the mighty possibilities lurking within you. Your unexplored capacity will cause trouble for you later. But if you develop and release it, it will bring you before great men.

GREAT POSSIBILITIES

Proverb 22:29 says;

> *Seest thou a man diligent in his business? he shall stand before kings; he shall not stand before mean men.*

Because the enemy knows you are destined for greatness he will try to attack you. He has insights to the brightness of your prospects in life.

When a child is born in Africa, they will take the child to a witchdoctor and check the person's destiny (i.e., the future of the person) and the children of the devil would see it and 99 percent of it is always correct. The enemy can see your star when you cannot see your own star. It is a tragedy for you to have divine investments and you are completely unaware.

There was a brother who was unhappy and he felt depressed. Yet he was a child of God. He went to his friend to complain. They were in the same church. The friend decided to take him to one fetish priest. He opined that everything is not all about church. When they got to the witchdoctor, he told him to stay outside and he said, "why? But, I came for help". The man said, "Tell him to stay outside". So the man went out. The witch-doctor now warned the friend not to bring that kind of person to him again because he had fire in him, and since he had fire in him, you don't bring such people here, because They will spoil our fetish power". The witchdoctor told the friend to tell him to go back to where he received fire. He made it categorically by clear that it was only that place that would solve the problem. But his friend could not deliver the message, so the witch-doctor went to the brother standing outside and said, "You have fire. People like you do not come to us. Go back to where you received your fire and your problems will be solved".

COSTLY IGNORANCE

Here was a believer, who had the fire of the Holy Spirit within. He had divine investments in him but he did not know. He wanted to cast his pearls before pigs and they threw him out. That is why the Bible says, in Psalm 49:20,

> *Man that is in honour, and understandeth not, is like the beasts that perish.*

Many of you running around for prayers from fake prophets if you develop your inner investment, you will discover that you are 100 percent better than those so called prophets.

Take a moment to pray aggressively.

Whether it is convenient for my enemy or not, my capacity must manifest, in the name of Jesus.

Capacity can be demoted or disturbed. It can also be dominated by the enemy. It can be downgraded. It can be disgraced. It can be diverted. It can be dismantled. Unfortunately it can be buried. It can be caged, it can be disillusioned. It can be defeated. It can be deadened, it can be deceased. Unfortunately capacity can be discouraged. It can be drained. It can be dribbled. It can be disoriented. It can be frustrated. It can be rendered null and void. It can be manipulated. It can be rendered useless. It can be blocked.

Prayer Points ←————————

1. Woe unto the demonic vessel, that the enemy would use to cause me spiritual injury, in the name of Jesus.

2. Father Lord, let your glory cover every aspect of my life, in the name of Jesus.

3. Father Lord, let your angels encamp around me, in Jesus' name.

4. I renounce and break every death covenant that I have made or which anyone has made on my behalf, in Jesus' name.

5. I remove the control of my life from the hands of any dead person, in the name of Jesus.

6. I stand against every covenant of sudden death, in Jesus' name.

CHAPTER 4

Prayers
To Block
Capacity
BLOCKERS

There are capacity blockers working against the release of many people's inner abilities. The reason we read about David today was because he overcame capacity blockers. There are capacity blockers assigned to ensure that many do not fulfill the agenda of God for their lives on earth. We need to identify what they are: -

1.   **The first capacity blocker is SIN:** Any sin in your life will strengthen the enemy to give you a hard fight. No matter what name you call yourself, if you are still living in sin, you cannot fulfill your capacity. Samson's destiny was derailed because of sin and it was blocked. There is no small sin. Sin is sin. Sin is terrible, ugly and bad. That is why Jesus usually said, "sin no more". The pastor may not see you commiting any sin. You may even be so clever as to conceal it. But eventually that sin will find you out.

Numbers 32:23

> *But if ye will not do so, behold, ye have sinned against the LORD: and be sure your sin will find you out.*

2. The second capacity blocker is **AIMLESSNESS.** When somebody is living an aimless life, no focus, no goal, no aim, such a person's capacity will be blocked. You must fight against aimlessness

Philippians 3:14-15

> *I press toward the mark for the prize of the high calling of God in Christ Jesus. Let us therefore, as many as be perfect, be thus minded: and if in any thing ye be otherwise minded, God shall reveal even this unto you.*

3. The third capacity blocker is the **SPIRIT OF SLUMBER.** When sleep has overtaken your prayer life and sleep has caged your life, you are living in the world of slumber.

Ephesians 5:14-17

> *Wherefore he saith, Awake thou that sleepest, and arise from the dead, and Christ shall give thee light. See then that ye walk circumspectly, not as fools, but as wise, Redeeming the time, because the days are evil. Wherefore be ye not unwise, but understanding what the will of the Lord is.*

4.   The fourth capacity blocker is **DISCOURAGEMENT.** When you get easily discouraged, you block your own capacity. You must overcome discouragement.

1Sam 30:1-6

> *And it came to pass, when David and his men were come to Ziklag on the third day, that the Amalekites had invaded*

the south, and Ziklag, and smitten Ziklag, and burned it with fire; And had taken the women captives, that were therein: they slew not any, either great or small, but carried them away, and went on their way. So David and his men came to the city, and, behold, it was burned with fire; and their wives, and their sons, and their daughters, were taken captives. Then David and the people that were with him lifted up their voice and wept, until they had no more power to weep. And David's two wives were taken captives, Ahinoam the Jezreelitess, and Abigail the wife of Nabal the Carmelite. And David was greatly distressed; for the people spake of stoning him, because the soul of all the people was grieved, every man for his sons and for his daughters: but David encouraged himself in the LORD his God.

5.   The fifth capacity blocker is **ANGER**. Anyone with the spirit of anger has a serious problems indeed. In fact, if anger is in your life, your problem is worse than the problems of all the witches in Nigeria put together. The Bible says;

Eccl 7:9

> *Be not hasty in thy spirit to be angry: for anger resteth in the bosom of fools.*

6.   The sixth capacity blocker is **TALKATIVENESS.** Having no control over your mouth is a mark of immaturity.

Eccl 5:2

> *Be not rash with thy mouth, and let not thine heart be hasty to utter any thing before God: for God is in heaven, and thou upon earth: therefore let thy words be few.*

7. The seventh capacity blocker is **NEGATIVE ENVIRONMENT.** An environment that is not convenient for your destiny. A place you have been for many years and your life did not change nor move forward can be said to be a negative environment.

8. The eight capacity blocker is **WRONG ASSOCIATION.** Wrong friends, wrong companions, can block your capacity. Beware of destiny killers.

1Cor 15:33-34

Be not deceived: evil communications corrupt good manners. Awake to righteousness, and sin not; for some have not the knowledge of God: I speak this to your shame.

9. The nineth capacity blocker is **MAKING HASTE.** Avoid making haste when you do not know where to go. You do

not know the direction, but you are rushing? The front is not clear and you are rushing? It blocks people's capacity.

Proverb 14:29

He that is slow to wrath is of great understanding: but he that is hasty of spirit exalteth folly.

10.   The tenth capacity blocker is a **CURSE**. A curse can limit a man seriously. It can block the capacity of a destiny completely. That is why you should not joke with curses issued on you. Remember;   Proverb 26:2, which says;

As the bird by wandering, as the swallow by flying, so the curse causeless shall not come.

11.   The eleventh capacity blocker is **UNBELIEF**. When you lack faith in God you block your capacity. You must get rid of every form of doubt and unbelief.

Mark 9:24

> *And straightway the father of the child cried out, and said with tears, Lord, I believe; help thou mine unbelief.*

Hebrew 3:12

> *Take heed, brethren, lest there be in any of you an evil heart of unbelief, in departing from the living God.*

12. The twelveth capacity blocker is **LAZINESS.** Many believers unfortunately are very lazy. Many are too lazy to pray, and too lazy to seek out things they want for themselves.

Proverb 26:13-16

> *The slothful man saith, There is a lion in the way; a lion is in the streets. As the door turneth upon his hinges, so doth the slothful upon his bed.*

The slothful hideth his hand in his bosom; it grieveth him to bring it again to his mouth. The sluggard is wiser in his own conceit than seven men that can render a reason.

13.   The thirteenth capacity blocker is **EVIL COVENANTS.** If you are from a family where they made a covenant not to move ahead or forward, it will affect you. Such evil covenant must be broken.

14.   The fouteenth capacity blocker is **PRIDE.** When you over value yourself. Nobody can talk to you. You believe that you know everything or you have all the knowledge. You will block your capacity.

Proverb 16:18

> *Pride goeth before destruction, and an haughty spirit before a fall.*

Prayer Points ←

1. I command every blockage in my spiritual pipe to be removed, in the name of Jesus.
2. I command the hole in my spiritual pipe to be closed, in the name of Jesus.
3. Lord, ignite my calling with Your fire, in the name of Jesus.
4. I receive heavenly flushing in my spiritual pipe, in Jesus' name.
5. Every evil spiritual padlock and evil chain hindering my spiritual growth, be roasted, in the name of Jesus.
6. I rebuke every spirit of spiritual deafness and blindness in my life, in the name of Jesus.
7. I bind the strongman behind my spiritual blindness and deafness and paralyse his operations in my life, in the name of Jesus.
8. I anoint my eyes and my ears, in the name of Jesus.
9. Lord, restore my spiritual eyes and ears, in the name of Jesus.

CHAPTER 5

Capacity Blockers must be *DISGRACED*

In this chapter we shall learn how to further wage war on stubborn capacity blockers. There are different levels of capacity blockers. There is a group of progress blockers that must be identified and disgraced.

1   **UNWILLINGNESS TO CHANGE.** God is saying, "change" but you are unwilling to change. One sign of insanity is to continue to do the same things and expect to get a different result.

Gal 6:7-8

Be not deceived; God is not mocked: for whatsoever a man soweth, that shall he also reap. For he that soweth to his flesh shall of the flesh reap corruption; but he that soweth to the Spirit shall of the Spirit reap life everlasting.

2.   **IGNORANCE OF SPIRITUAL WARFARE.** If you do not know that you have a battle to fight, you are swimming in the ocean of ignorance.

3.   **SELF SATISFACTION.** You are satisfied with where you are. You do not want any body to change you. You do not want anybody to talk to you. Self satisfaction can tie the hands of God. But God will always respond to the hungry and the desperate. If He sees that you are hungry and desperate, he will respond to you.

Proverb 3:7

Be not wise in thine own eyes: fear the LORD, and depart from evil.

Romans 12:6

Having then gifts differing according to the grace that is given to us, whether prophecy, let us prophesy according to the proportion of faith;

4. **POWERS OF YOUR FATHER'S HOUSE.** When the powers of your father's house are troubling your destiny, you will encounter lots of setbacks. You need deliverance.

5. **DISTRACTIONS.** Distractions mainly look important but they are 'fake' opportunities. Distraction is a very powerful weapon of the enemy. It is even easy to come to church and be distracted. That is why we tell people that when you come to the house of God, "looking unto Jesus is the key". Do not look at the pastor. Do not look at anybody. Look unto Jesus.

6. **BEING CONTROLLED BY THE FLESH.** When the flesh is controlling your life. All the moodiness, depression, self centeredness, indiscipline, stubbornness, idolatry, covetousness are works of the flesh.

John 6:63

> *It is the spirit that quickeneth; the flesh profiteth nothing: the words that I speak unto you, they are spirit, and they are life.*

7. **SATANIC STRONGHOLD.** A stronghold is a position in a territory that devil has occupied. A position of power that the enemy is using. A fortress of the enemy. When you begin to do certain things you strengthen the stronghold of the enemy against you. A lot of men and women are inside the strongholds of capacity blockers now. They have eaten the food on the table of the devil. They have had sex with possessed persons. They have been consulting with false prophets. They have all kind of incisions on their bodies. And these have blocked them completely.

2Cor 10:4-6

> *(For the weapons of our warfare are not carnal, but mighty through God to the pulling down of strong holds;)*

Casting down imaginations, and every high thing that exalteth itself against the knowledge of God, and bringing into captivity every thought to the obedience of Christ; And having in a readiness to revenge all disobedience, when your obedience is fulfilled.

Today, I pray that you will be completely released from all these blockers, in the name of Jesus.

This is why many christians suffer the same defeat, over and over again. Because what is meant to move them forward has not been utilised.

What do you need to do?

1.   Be born again; surrender your life to God.

2.   Be free permanently from sin.

3.   You need to pray battle prayers.

This book is a prophetic book and it is also a warfare book. If you will pray from your heart, your life will change. Then, you will begin to realise where you should go, that you are not going. Where you should throw your net, that you are not throwing your net. Those you should talk with that you are not taking with. Those things you should do but because, you do not exercise, you could not do them. There are many people who have hidden talents within, but have buried their capacity. Many people have the internal Moses that could deliver this generation but what a tragedy when you subject your internal Moses to a boxing match. You are the one fighting your Moses And therefore, your Moses cannot do much for you.

BE FREE!

There are people who are priceless treasures but buried by witchcraft. There are people, that should be landlords but they are still tenants. There are some men and women, if not for careless sex which they had in the past, they would have become great men and women. It means that the enemy has completely blocked their capacity.

The people of Israel did not fulfill their capacity. They said, "We cannot enter the promised land because there are giants there," and they did not enter. Samson did not fulfill his capacity. Saul's capacity was blocked, so he could not move. He was the man appointed to be the king of Israel. He started his journey by prophecies but he ended up as a witch. If you keep quiet, you are finished. A closed mouth is a closed destiny.

Prayer Points

1. Every power, blocking my capacity, your time is up, die, in the name of Jesus.
2. Pharaoh of my father's house, let me go, in the name of Jesus.
3. I must excel, I must manifest, in the name of Jesus.
4. Any bird that wants to pick my breakthroughs, die, in the name of Jesus.
5. Power of the tail, over my destiny, die, in the name of Jesus.
6. Every power, assigned to bury me alive, die, in the name of Jesus.

7. Every power assigned against my joy, die, in the name of Jesus.

8. Father in the name of Jesus, I lift up myself into your hands, whether it is convenient for any power or not, I will arise, in Jesus' name.

9. Beginning from now, I bury every power blocking my capacity, in the name of Jesus.

10. I receive the oil of favour, in the name of Jesus.

11. I will reach where I am supposed to reach, in the name of Jesus.

12. My time of maximum lifting up has come, in the name of Jesus.

13. Any power, sitting on my moving forward, be unseated now and for ever, in the name of Jesus.

14. Any power saying, "Over their dead body" will I have my full scale laughter, be scattered, in the name of Jesus.

15. In my dreams, oh God, appear, in the name of Jesus.

16. The same way the enemy has blocked my life, that same way will they go back and die, in the name of Jesus.

CHAPTER 6

Power
for *Explosive*
SUCCESS

Success is achieving all that God created you to achieve. Success is prospering in every area of your life. Success is discovering your best talents, skills and abilities and applying them to make the most effective contribution to your fellow men. Success, as far as the Bible is concerned, is the achievement of God's goals and purpose in your life. Success is doing those things God has ordained you to do and doing them in a way that would satisfy God. Success is to positively contribute to the betterment of others. Success is doing God's will.

Success is what you do with your potentials. It is accomplishing your set goals in life. It is good journey towards your goals. Success is the development of your untapped potentials. Success is ability to spend your life in God's own way. Unfortunately there are many living their lives the way it was not written about them.

Success is activating your inner power house. Unto every man brought to this world is a power house given by God. Your power house may be your hands.

It may be your brain, your voice or the way you hold yourself. Your power house may be your mental capacity. Success is activating your inner power house. Your power house may be your virtues, that you need to activate to bring you what God wants to bring you.

2 Chronicles 26:15

> *And he made in Jerusalem engines, invented by cunning men, to be on the towers and upon the bulwarks, to shoot arrows and great stones withal. And his name spread far abroad; for he was marvellously helped, till he was strong.*

My prayer for you is that may heaven help you marvellously in Jesus name. Everyone in life who is not a sick man or mentally derailed man, wants to be successful in life. But many do not understand what success entails or requires.

THE ENVIRONMENT

It has been well said by our ancient fathers that there can never be any blessing for the fish that has decided to go to the tree. Success is to leave the world better than you found it. Success is recording accomplishments beyond your wildest dream. Success is thinking of yesterday without regret and thinking of tomorrow without fear. Success is making chariot wheels of all your difficulties. Success is the maximum utilisation of your ability. Success is bouncing back when you hit the bottom. Success is making your life a masterpiece such that you stand in the presence of God and you are not ashamed at all. Success is to know where you are going and to go there and fulfill the purpose of God for your life.

However it is important to know that success in life is achieved through strategic empowerment. You will receive some extra abilities to be your best in life.

Many people know about success. Many people desire success but never attain it because of some limitations and constraints. However through the supernatural and enabling power of the Holy Spirit, you can overcome all obstacles and reach your goals in life.

Declare this loud "My Father empower me to succeed by the power in the blood of Jesus.

THE BIBLE SAYS

This book of the law shall not depart out of thy mouth; but thou shalt meditate therein day and night, that thou mayest observe to do according to all that is written therein: for then thou shalt make thy way prosperous, and then thou shalt have good success. Joshua 1:8

Many who are successful in life and who have attained greatness in life can testify of spiritual abilities that enable them to become great. Joshua gave himself to the word of God and he became great in life. Through the supernatural power of God, he divided river Jordan and Israel passed over to take their inheritance. God assigned a special angel to him. From the time that special angel was with Joshua, the war of inheritance over Canaan was just a walkover. I pray that the angel that will empower you for success shall resume duty in the name of Jesus.

GOD OF POSSIBILITIES

Success that is achieved is not only by dint of hard-work or by natural means. You need to be spiritually backed up. There are plenty of talented men who are complete failures. There are plenty of intelligent people who are complete failures. You need divine assistance and empowerment.

David was a bundle of success and he had great achievement. He was anointed and empowered by God to rule and to prevail over the enemy. He got a great name in Israel. Moses was a stammerer who ran away from Pharaoh because the king of Egypt wanted to kill him. However, when God met him by the burning bush in the desert, He empowered him and he became like a 'god' to Pharaoh. With that rod in the hand of Moses, he rescued the children of Israel from the hand of Pharaoh. You shall be a 'god' to your Pharaoh, in Jesus' name.

Paul the apostle was somebody who persecuted the saints. He too was saved and empowered to deliver the gentiles. Eventually he finished well and he wrote more than half of the books in the New Testament. He attributed his success to empowerment from God.

What are the different ways of divine empowerment to succeed?

1. **Through walking with God.** God is the primary source of light, power and grace to succeed. The Bible says, "In Him was life and this life was the light of men". When you walk with God you cannot fail. You cannot be unsuccessful, for God will lead you to the place of greatness and breakthrough. The trouble is, we do our walk with God haphazardly. Some people only pray very well when they are happy.

That time you went on holidays in prayer school, the enemy will use it to run faster into your life.

2.   **You can be empowered through the word of God.** The word of God is the light that lightens our way. The Bible says the word of God is quick and powerful, sharper than any two edged sword. When you believe in that word of God and you practise it, you will have good success.

3.   **You can be empowered through righteousness.** Righteousness exalts a nation, but sin is a reproach to any people. Righteousness will facilitate your greatness. Sin will lead to failure and ridicule. Righteousness is a defence and it has a voice that speaks on your defence to defend you. But sin opens the door of destruction unto people's life.

4.   **You can be empowered through the baptism of the Holy Ghost and by**

receiving spiritual gifts. Every believer should seek to be baptised with the Holy Ghost and spiritual gifts.

5.   Through violent faith. When you seek God, you must believe that He is and He is a rewarder of those who diligently seek Him.

6.   **You can be empowered through prayers**. There is nothing that cannot be achieved through prayer.

7.   **You can be empowered through the intervention of ministering spirits.** Angels of God are called ministering spirits. They are sent forth to minister to the saints of God. They have assisted plenty of believers to be successful. Even Jesus our master received angelic assistance. Angelic assistance also released Peter from jail. Angelic assistance also helped King Hezekiah destroy the Assyrians. At all times, we need the supernatural assistance of ministering spirits.

8. **We can be empowered through visions, revelations and divine ideas.** You need to have a Joseph's dream. You need to have revelation on what to do. You need divine revelation from heaven that will make you shine and overtake those who have gone before you.

"Thus saith the LORD, thy Redeemer, the Holy One of Israel; I am the LORD thy God which teacheth thee to profit, which leadeth thee by the way that thou shouldest go." Isaiah 48:17

9. **You can be empowered through diligence and hard work.** The Bible says, "Seeth thou a man who is diligent in his work, he will stand before kings. He will not stand before mean men".

10. **You can be empowered through brokenness.** When you are completely broken you become a member of the

council of heaven. God makes you a favourite person. He will confide in you and talk with you.

"Surely the Lord GOD will do nothing, but he revealeth his secret unto his servants the prophets." Amos 3:7

Prayer Points ←——————

1. Lord, give unto me, the key to good success, so that anywhere I go, the doors of good success will be opened unto me.
2. Lord, let the anointing to excel in my spiritual and physical life, fall on me, in Jesus' name.
3. I reject the anointing of nonachievement in my handiwork, in the name of Jesus.
4. Let all those circulating my name for evil, be disgraced, in the name of Jesus.

5.   Let all evil friends make mistakes that will expose them, in the name of Jesus.

6.   I refuse to wear the garment of tribulation and sorrow, in the name of Jesus.

7.   Lord, let the spirit that flees from sin, incubate my life.

8.   Lord, produce in me, the power of self-control and gentleness.

9.   I loose. . . from the bondage the powers of darkness placed on him or her by the blood of the Lord Jesus Christ.

10. By the blood of Jesus, I cancel and render null and void, all commands issued by the powers of darkness in . . .'s life, in the name of Jesus.

OTHER PUBLICATIONS BY DR. D. K. OLUKOYA

29.   Deliverance: God's Medicine Bottle
30.   Destiny Clinic
31.   Destroying Satanic Masks
32.   Disgracing Soul Hunters
33.   Divine Military Training
34.   Divine Yellow Card
35.   Dominion Prosperity
36.   Drawers Of Power From The Heavenlies
37.   Evil Appetite
38.   Evil Umbrella
39.   Facing Both Ways
40.   Failure In The School Of Prayer
41.   Fire For Life's Journey
42.   For We Wrestle ...
43.   Freedom Indeed
44.   Holiness Unto The Lord
45.   Holy Cry
46.   Holy Fever
47.   Hour Of Decision
48.   How To Obtain Personal Deliverance
49.   How To Pray When Surrounded By The Enemies
50.   Idols Of The Heart
51.   Is This What They Died For?
52.   Let God Answer By Fire
53.   Limiting God
54.   Madness Of The Heart
55.   Making Your Way Through The Traffic Jam of Life

YORUBA PUBLICATIONS

1. ADURA AGBAYORI
2. ADURA TI NSI OKE NIDI
3. OJO ADURA

FRENCH PUBLICATIONS

1. PLUIE DE PRIERE
2. ESPIRIT DE VAGABONDAGE
3. EN FINIR AVEC LES FORCES MALEFIQUES DE LA MAISON DE TON PERE
4. QUE l'ENVOUTEMENT PERISSE
5. FRAPPEZ l'ADVERSAIRE ET IL FUIRA
6. COMMENT RECEVIOR LA DELIVRANCE DU MARI ET FEMME DE NUIT
7. CPMMENT SE DELIVRER SOI-MEME
8. POVOIR CONTRE LES TERRORITES SPIRITUEL
9. PRIERE DE PERCEES POUR LES HOMMES D'AFFAIRES
10. PRIER JUSQU'A REMPORTER LA VICTOIRE
11. PRIERES VIOLENTES POUR HUMILIER LES PROBLEMES OPINIATRES
12. PRIERE POUR DETRUIRE LES MALADIES ET INFIRMITES
13. LE COMBAT SPIRITUEL ET LE FOYER
14. BILAN SPIRITUEL PERSONNEL
15. VICTOIRES SUR LES REVES SATANIQUES
16. PRIERES DE COMAT CONTRE 70 ESPIRITS DECHANINES
17. LA DEVIATION SATANIQUE DE LA RACE NOIRE
18. TON COMBAT ET TA STRATEGIE
19. VOTRE FONDEMENT ET VOTRE DESTIN
20. REVOQUER LES DECRETS MALEFIQUES
21. CANTIQUE DES CONTIQUES

22. LE MAUVAIS CRI DES IDOLES
23. QUAND LES CHOSES DEVIENNENT DIFFICILES
24. LES STRATEGIES DE PRIERES POUR LES CELIBATAIRES
25. SE LIBERER DES ALLIANCES MALEFIQUES
26. DEMANTELER LA SORCELLERIE
27. LA DELIVERANCE: LE FLACON DE MEDICAMENT DIEU
28. LA DELIVERANCE DE LA TETE
29. COMMANDER LE MATIN
30. NE GRAND MAIS LIE
31. POUVOIR CONTRE LES DEMOND TROPICAUX
32. LE PROGRAMME DE TRANFERT DE RICHESSE
33. LES ETUDIANTS A l'ECOLE DE LA PEUR
34. L'ETOILE DANS VOTRE CIEL
35. LES SAISONS DE LA VIE
36. FEMME TU ES LIBEREE

ANNUAL 70 DAYS PRAYER AND FASTING PUBLICATIONS

1. Prayers That Bring Miracles
2. Let God Answer By Fire
3. Prayers To Mount With Wings As Eagles
4. Prayers That Bring Explosive Increase
5. Prayers For Open Heavens
6. Prayers To Make You Fulfil Your Divine Destiny
7. Prayers That Make God To Answer And Fight By Fire.

8. Prayers That Bring Unchallengeable Victory And Breakthrough Rainfall Bombardments
9. Prayers That Bring Dominion Prosperity And Uncommon Success
10. Prayers That Bring Power And Overflowing Progress
11. Prayers That Bring Laughter And Enlargement Breakthroughs
12. Prayers That Bring Uncommon Favour And Breakthroughs
13. Prayers That Bring Unprecedented Greatness & Unmatchable Increase
14. Prayers That Bring Awesome Testimonies And Turn Around Breakthroughs.

BOOKS BY PASTOR (MRS) SHADE OLUKOYA

1. Power To Fulfil Your Destiny
2. Principles Of A Successful Marriage
3. The Call of God
4. The Daughters of Phillip
5. When Your Destiny is Under Attack
6. Violence Against Negative Voices
7. Woman of Wonder
8. I Decree An Uncommon Change